I0472551

Accounting Information Systems

An Essential Guide for Beginners

Y.K.Wong, Ph.D.

Production:

Book submission: 11 Aug 2016

Book revision: 17 Oct 2016

Final acceptance: 30 Dec 2016

First editorial services submission: 12 Jan 2016

Second editorial services submission: 18 Jan 2016

Cover image: 18 Dec 2016

Online version: 18 Dec 2016

Print version: 18 Jan 2017

Revision: 21 Jan 2017

Description

Accounting plays a critical role in any business or organization. With the rapid growth of business financial transactions and the advancement of technology, accounting information systems are dominant in supporting all accounting functions and business transactions in society today. Traditional accounting operational roles are now fully managed by accounting information systems. This book provides practical approaches to everything you need to know about accounting information systems. It covers basic accounting principles, characteristics and deployment strategies of accounting information systems, accounting cycles, risks, and control strategies for accounting information systems.

This book also offers a Certificate of Completion and instructor test bank. It is an essential guide for all beginners.

Keywords: accounting, information systems, basic, beginner

About the Author

Y.K. Wong holds a Ph.D. in Computing Science from the University of Technology, Sydney, Australia. She received her Master's degree in Advanced Information Systems and Management from The University of New South Wales, Australia, and a Bachelor of Commerce from Curtin University of Technology, Australia.

Dr. Wong has produced quality publications (books, journals, and referred conference papers). Her first book, titled 'Modern Software Review: Techniques and Technology', was published in 2006. She is the Associate Editor for the International Review of Business Research and the International Journal of PIE (an A-list journal), consulting editor for Australian Journal on Information Systems, and reviewer (scholarly peer-reviewed) for many top-tier journals such as IEEE, AIS, and various A-list journals. She served in the Technical Committee for International Association of Science and Technology for Development between 2006 and 2009, the Academic Advocate for ISACA between 2013 and 2015, and the program and track chairs for several conferences such as the Global Business and Social Science Research Conference in 2014 and Pacific Asia Conference on Information Systems in 2008. She has been actively engaged with professional bodies including the Association for Information Systems Special Interest Group on IT/IS in Asia Pacific (AIS-SIG IT/IS), The International of Association for Accounting Education and Research (IAAER), Project Management Institute (PMI), Academy of Management (AOM), The Information Systems Audit and Control Association (ISACA), IEEE Communications Society (IEEE Communication), ACM Special Interest Group: Mobile (SIG Mobile), and Certified Public Accounting (CPA).

Dr. Wong is a consultant, researcher, and teacher in various universities and international companies. She taught at the University of New South Wales, Griffith University, the University of Technology, Sydney, and the University of Southern Queensland in the areas of business and information technology between 2001 and 2014. She has been teaching Accounting Information Systems and Auditing since 2010. Prior to her academic appointments, she worked in the areas of enterprise resources planning systems implementation systems and business processes re-engineering, e-commerce solutions, logistics, operations, and procurement; sales and marketing and product development since 1991.

Contents

Chapter 1

Accounting Information Systems

Accounting information systems (AIS) are designed for small to large enterprise businesses. Accounting professionals provide several types of support, including accounting operations (e.g., transaction processing, accounts receivable and payable, and internal reporting), external reporting (e.g., statutory reporting, corporate finance, financial risk, regulation and compliance with regulations, audit, and taxes), strategic accounting management (e.g., forecasting, budgeting, costing, reporting, cash flow management, financial performance, strategic decision supports, benchmarking, and various accounting-related managing activities) (Axelsen et al., 2017; Collier, 2015; Bol et al., 2016; Apostolou et al., 2014).

Since AIS have been widely adopted in the last two decades, the trend of accounting practice has shifted from traditional accounting operational support to strategic and control management. The accounting practice trend further concentrates the risks and security controls after the 2008 financial crisis (Coyne et al., 2016). The results from a survey conducted by Chartered Institute Management Accounting in early 2010 to benchmark the accounting practice worldwide (Stede and Malone, 2010) suggested three major categories of accounting operations: transaction processing, accounting operations, and accounts payable and receivable. Internal and external reporting have been computerized using accounting information systems. More companies now use accounting information systems for accounting operations and transaction processing support, and as such, the demand of financial accounting roles has been reduced (Axelsen et al., 2017; Apostolou et al., 2014).

With the wide adoption of accounting information systems and Computer Assisted Auditing Tools and Techniques (CAATTs), better risk management and controls can be carried out by auditors (Mayberry, 2013). Nowadays, auditors can continuously monitor accounting activities such as errors, fraud detection, analytical data reporting, and interactive reporting. The trend accounting practices has towards strategic accounting management support and auditing focuses on ways to improve the efficiency and effectiveness of audit procedures, risk management, and controls (Axelsen et al., 2017; Bol et al., 2016)).

What is an Accounting Information System?
An AIS aims to collect, process, store, and report financial data that can be used by managers, accountants, tax agencies, shareholders, and any other internal and external parties for decision making (Fawcett and Martin, 2016). The AIS is a core knowledge area in the accounting discipline and is an important requirement for accounting practice. AISs can be used to support all accounting functions and activities, including financial reporting, auditing, taxation, and management accounting (Axelsen et al., 2017).

AISs were introduced in the early 1970s for payroll functions (Wong, 2017). At the time, many accounting functions were executed manually, which could be ineffective and inefficient (Bol et al., 2016). AISs automate the processing of large amounts of data and produce timely and accurate information. Nowadays, two widely adopted accounting modules using AISs are auditing and financial reporting. With the advanced and rapid growth of information technology and process improvements, the AISs can provide full services to support all functional areas of financial accounting, managerial (management) accounting, taxation, and auditing (Axelsen et al., 2017).

The main components of an AIS are data, software, information technology infrastructure, and internal controls. Procedures and instructions can be automated. By adopting middleware, analytic tools, and user-friendly computer-interface designs, users (e.g., accountants and managers) can easily retrieve accounting information from an AIS (Bol et al., 2016).

The accounting functions give measurements, processing and communicating financial information about the business entities. As such, AISs are computerized to support a full range of accounting functions. Understanding business cycles and processes is critical to the success of the accounting functions.

Characteristics of Accounting Information Systems
Key characteristics of AISs are (Collier, 2015; Fawcett and Martin, 2016; Fang and Shu, 2016; Bol et al., 2016; Turner, 2013):

- AISs capture data and produce financial statements and reports. This process generally refers to the transaction processing system, which deals with day-to-day business transactions and operations.

- AISs produce financial information that can be used for both external and internal users. The internal users are business managers, who use the accounting information for planning, budgeting, and controls, while external users are customers, shareholders, vendors, investors, stock exchanges, and statutory authorities.

- AISs are designed for accounting functions. In financial accounting functions, an AIS is designed for and complies with the Generally Accepted Accounting Principles (GAAP), International Financial Reporting Standards (IFRS), International Accounting Standards Board (IASB), and relevant local and international standards to produce relevant financial statements. Three key components of financial statements are cash flow, profit and loss, and financial position, which can all be produced by AISs.

- AISs produce financial reports based on historical data and internal sources (business transactions). Financial information and statements can be used for various purposes (Bol et al., 2016).

- The financial information produced by the AISs should be identical to that produced by the manual approach. The optimal goals of the AIS are to provide efficiency and effective operations and to produce error-free financial statements and reports. The financial statements are used by external and internal users.

- AISs provide greater security management and controls. With appropriately deployed security and defense strategies, they can reduce faults and crime (Bol et al., 2016). However, this also introduces a need for cyber security and management.

- AISs can provide backups of master files to maintain a higher level of data integrity and security.

Characteristics of Accounting Information
Accounting information can be characterized as relevant, reliable, complete, timely, understandable, verifiable, and accessible (Collier, 20015; Fang and Shu, 2016; Bol et al.):

- Accessible—information must be available and obtainable.
- Complete—information must be sufficient to allow users to make decisions.
- Relevant—information can be used to help make decisions.
- Reliable—information must be free of errors and bias.
- Timing—information timing is critical to making decisions.
- Understandable—information must be presented in a way that users can easily interpret.
- Verifiable—information must be consistently traceable with errors and bias.

There are several advantages of AISs, including improving the quality of information and reducing human errors for large transactions. It also can reduce long-term costs, particularly with a high volume of transactions and operational costs. AISs can significantly improve internal controls by reducing human risk, particularly when organizations deal with financial data (Collier, 2015). Overall, AISs can produce timely and accurate data on which users can base decisions (Bol et al., 2016).

Chapter 2

Accounting Information System Development Strategies

There are three common ways to adopt an AIS. These developments are mainly focused either "buy" or "build." In terms of the system development, the common ways are (Drum et al., 2017; Turner; 2013; Smith and Smith, 2016):

- Buy an AIS
- In-house development
- Appoint an external firm to build and maintain

There are three goals that need to be considered for developing an accounting information system (Hall, 2015; Laudon and Laudon, 2015; Smith and Smith, 2016):

1. To meet the regulatory and statutory reporting requirements
2. To provide effective and reliable accounting information to relevant users
3. To protect accounting data and avoid all possible risks or security breaches.

Buying an AIS

For a small company with basic computer systems, one of the options would be commercial off-the-self (COTS) software. Many of these AIS software packages are designed for small businesses for financial accounting and reporting. Implementing COTS software requires software training for all users (Laudon and Laudon, 2015). The existing information technology infrastructure also must be compatible with the COTS software (Singh, 2016; Filasrae et al., 2016). Data management, storage, and system maintenance are done locally and the costs are generally low.

Another option is to purchase a turnkey computer system where customized software and hardware are often included as a package, also referred to as appliance (Hayek et al., 2014). The turnkey computer system package is simple and easy to use. A turnkey computer system includes hardware, software, operating system and all associated applications that are customized to the business requirements (Laudon and Laudon, 2015). There is no requirement to build or change the existing information technology infrastructure. Data storage and system maintenance are done locally and costs vary depending on the business and system requirements (Smith and Smith, 2016).

The final option is to buy a service via an application services provider (ASP); many internet companies (or cloud-based) providers can lease accounting software via the internet. This requires internet services and web-browsers. The cloud computing services provide user-friendly system, back-up and customer services support function. However, control and storage of financial data, which are managed and held by the external ASP, are limited for users (Smith and Smith, 2016).

Build in-house

Building a new AIS is another option other than buying software. This method often requires additional and/or change of current Information Technology infrastructure. This option is normally suitable to larger companies that already have an IT development team. Traditionally, many companies use this tailored approach to build an AIS (Laudon and Laudon, 2015). The major advantage of this approach is that it allows the company to fully control and design an AIS according to its business preferences.

Many in-house developments involve input from end-users during the development cycle, including the prototyping phase. Using an end-user development approach generally provides tailored systems according to users' preferences. The prototyping approach can build a sub-set of the systems with the involvement of the end-users during the system development life cycle. However, there are a number of risk factors for the building in-house approach, such as a longer time for development and implementation, higher costs, poorer documentations of the AIS system, competency of in-house developers, possible requirements to change business structures, changes of the business process, internal politics, cooperation among the departments, concerns of the internal controls, and support of top management (Smith and Smith, 2016).

Outsource

Outsourcing is a very common way for larger companies to adopt an AIS. This requires the hiring of an external software company to complete the development and implementation of the AIS. The outsourced software company usually has expertise in the domain area and it provides consulting (pre-sale and after-sale) services and handles all activities related to the AIS (Laudon and Laudon, 2015). This can generally reduce the development cycle and improve documentation and planning.

The development costs could vary depending on costs from the outsourced company. The method used by the outsource company is the same as it would be if the AIS were built in-house. It includes business process review and redesign, prototyping, and use of computer-aided software engineering (CASE) tools to support the AIS development (Sutcliffe, 2016). The CASE is software that helps to analyze, plan, design, implement and maintain the AIS. Additional user training and Information Technology support staff are often required after development. Table 1 provides comparison of three common ways for adopting an AIS (Cassidy, 2016; Christ and Nicolaou, 2016; Ward and Peppard, 2016; Laudon and Laudon, 2015; Smith and Smith, 2016).

Table 2.1: Comparison

	Buy an AIS	**Build in-house**	**Outsource**
Size of company	Small-Medium	Medium-Large	Small-Large
Development costs	Low	High	Low-Medium
Maintenance costs	Low	High	Medium
Time	Short	Long	Medium
Changes of business process	Limited	High	Medium
Additional information technology infrastructure	No	Yes	Yes
Internal controls	Medium	Medium	Medium
User training requirements	Limited	High	High
Top management support	High	Low	Medium
Documentations	Low	Medium	High
Business restructure	Low	High	High
Users' cooperation	High	Low	Medium
Internal politics	Low	High	Medium
AIS scalability	Medium	Low	Medium

Chapter 3

Trend of Accounting Information Systems Adoption

In alignment with business operations and accounting practices, it is important to adopt appropriate technologies. In addition, due to the complexity and multifaceted dimensions of governance, partnership, value measurement, competency, communication, skill, and employees' incentives, a strategical approach to deploying the accounting information system can maximize benefits and return on investments. Research studies suggest that investment in accounting information systems by small and medium enterprises provides many advantages, such as efficiency in operations, a reduction in human errors and the cost of fixing errors, an increase in productivity, and an improvement in reporting quality (Drum et al., 2017; Laudon and Laudon, 2015).

Accounting Information Systems - Cloud computing

There are increasing numbers of cloud computing services in accounting information systems (Wong, 2017). The concept of cloud computing is to employ remote servers over the internet for processing, managing, and storing data. Often, users only use web-interface to connect the remote servers. This cloud computing architecture has been increasing in popularity for small and medium enterprises because the cost to set up and maintain it is low (Laudon and Laudon, 2015).

Most companies set contracts with service providers who can provide a full range of information technology support, from deployment to regular maintenance to upgrade services. Additionally, the use of cloud-based services doesn't require the installation of software onto local servers or users' computers, as the software is generally located and stored at the remote servers. This is also known as Software-as-a-Service (SaaS) (Belfo and

Trigo, 2013). Most SaaS service providers include full information technology training to users. Information technology support is offered by the service providers and is not required within the company (Bhimani and Willcocks, 2014). Many software companies such as NetSuite Financials, SAP ERP Financials, Microsoft Dynamics GP, SAGE, Intacct Financial and Accounting System, or SAGE provide accounting information systems using cloud computing architecture.

These service providers offer key components of accounting functions such as inventory management, core accounting, fund accounting, billing, invoicing, budgeting, forecasting, financial reporting, payroll management, human resources, project accounting, work order management, and fixed asset accounting. Some of the services also provide management accounting and auditing components (Axelsen et al., 2017). Benefits of deploying cloud computing include (Wong, 2017; Belfo and Trigo, 2013; Laudon and Laudon, 2015):

1. Easy and convenient for adoption when a company has limited expertise in information technology.
2. Low cost – most cloud computing service providers offer a range of competitive prices with a range of services.
3. Reduce in-house information technology services – contracting external providers can reduce in-house costs.
4. Decrease conflict of interests among departments – accounting units within the company remain independent.
5. Switching and upgrade costs are low – it is easy to change providers and upgrade the services.

However, the main disadvantage of cloud computing is that software and hardware are generally managed in remote locations by the cloud service provider. Data is stored by remote servers that are also managed by the cloud service provider. This option would be unattractive for a company that has slow internet connectivity or poor internet and web services.

Mobile and Wireless Technologies

With a rapid growth of mobile and wireless technologies, many companies have approachable bring your own (BYO) devices. By adopting mobile and wireless technologies, users can perform their work or access the data more easily. The convenient features of mobile and wireless technologies have significantly changed communication. For every 100 people in the world, there are 97 mobile cellular subscriptions, and a total of 6.9 billion phones are connected (Brahima, 2014; Wikipedia, 2016). The region with the highest mobile phone usage is Hong Kong, with 2.4 phones per person on average. The lowest is North Korea, with 0.08 phones per person on average.

The trend of BYO devices and using mobile and wireless technologies has become increasingly popular in the workforce (Wong, 2017; Laudon and Laudon, 2015). Many companies are accepting mobile workforces. With the requirements of international accounting associations and standardization practices, many companies will take advantage of world contracting and outsourcing functions. Accounting workforce trends will also shift; traditional full-time accountants will move to independent contracting roles.

Business Intelligence, Business Analytics and Big Data

The term of business intelligence (BI) can be defined as techniques or strategies to transform business raw data to meaningful information for strategical decision making (Bacic and Fadlalla, 2016). This is associated with large amounts of data, analytical tools (such as standardized statistical modelling and data mining), middleware, and information technologies (Sledgianowski et al., 2017). The overall objective is to simplify the data and transform it in a way that managers or users can easily interpret the information. In particular, this meaningful information allows users to identify opportunities and implement effective solutions.

Business intelligence is generally based on the historical data with a set of standardized modeling or reports from the traditional performance measurement methods (Turner, 2013). Traditional business intelligence is querying and reporting using online analytical processing (OLAP) (Stede and Malone, 2010). Many accounting information systems providers also provide a middleware feature.

With the development of business analytics, accountants can provide investigation, provide deeper business analysis, and understand business performance in a more comprehensive way. Business analytics is particularly useful to accountants for dealing with a large volume of data and applying different types of statistical modeling and data mining techniques to fulfill many business requirements. Business analytics apply advanced statistical and predictive modeling techniques, such as predictive modeling for forecasting (Laudon and Laudon, 2015).

Today, many business intelligence tools and techniques offer data mining, process and text mining, benchmarking, complex event processing, business performance matrix management, and predictive and prescriptive analytics (Bacic and Fadlalla, 2016; Sledgianowski et al., 2017).

These tools perfectly complement the role of many accountants who have shifted to take up positions that are more strategic and analytical in nature (Turner, 2013). Today, accountants play more important roles in strategic business reporting, decision making, and planning.

Big Data
There are increasingly more discussions regarding big data in accounting practice. Big data refers to data sets that require more advanced data processing, application, and analytical techniques due to their complexity and size (Sledgianowski et al., 2016; Laudon and Laudon, 2015). Accountants no longer just focus on small sets of accounting data and basic accounting operations. Rather, they deal with complex business problems and decision

making. Accountants are now facing larger and more complex accounting and financial data. The advancement of information technology allows the accountants to provide more next-level support for big data (Sledgianowski et al., 2017). For internal auditing, internal controls and risk management, big data become a challenge in maintaining compliance. Big data is important to accounting practice, particularly in dealing with complex business models and global businesses (Laudon and Laudon, 2015).

Chapter 4

Accounting Cycle

From the accounting perspective, practitioners are generally interested in business activities that relate to accounting. Fundamentally, accounting equations are formulated as follows:

Asset = (Revenue – Expenditure) + Liability

It can be written as

Asset – Liability = Revenue – Expenditure;
Revenues - Expenditure = Profit/Loss

Asset refers to the economic activities that provide future economic benefits. Profit and loss are the associated business activities that generate incomes or costs, respectively (that is a total amount of revenue minus a total amount of expenditures). Liabilities refer to a total cost that a company owes to others (e.g. borrowing from a bank) (Gelinas et al., 2014; Simkin et al., 2014).

In order to accurately record and report all financial data, accountants are particularly interested in business processes and transactions. An Accounting Information System provides system support for all accounting events and activities. The accounting cycle is a collective series of processes beginning with a transaction occurring and ending with its inclusion in the financial reporting. This interconnection between accounting activities and sequence of processes can be summarized into a single accounting cycle (Drum et al., 2017; Simkin et al., 2014).

The accounting cycle has a start and completion date within the accounting period. This period is a defined timeframe for financial reporting, such as monthly, quarterly, and annually. Figure 1 shows the accounting cycle, including transactions from source documents, journal entries, ledger accounts, trial balance, adjustments, financial statements (trading accounts, profit and loss, cash flow, balance sheet, statement of equity), closing entries, and post-closing trial balance (Drum et al., 2017; Apostolou et al., 2014; Gelinas et al., 2014; Smith and Smith, 2016; Simkin et al., 2014).

Figure 1- Accounting Cycle in Accounting Practice

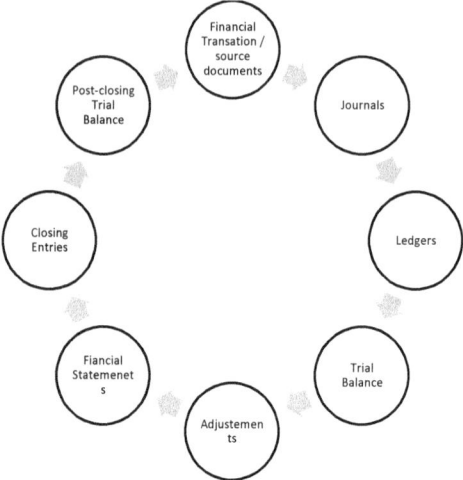

From the Accounting Information System view, Figure 2 shows the accounting cycle that includes revenue, expenditure, general ledger and other business cycles, such as Human Resource Management and Payroll (Drum et al., 2017; Apostolou et al., 2014; Simkin et al., 2014).

Figure 2: Accounting cycles in the Accounting Information System

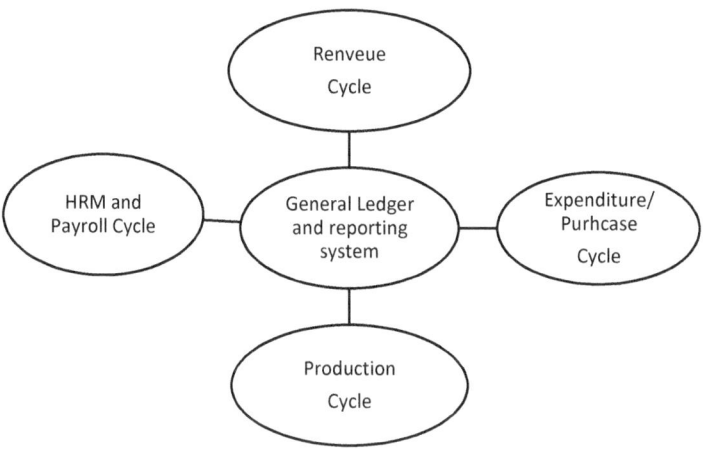

Risks and Controls

There are many risks and controls mechanisms in the accounting process. Different stakeholders such as managers, employees, shareholders, and customers might have different views in managing risks and controls. The Committee of Sponsoring Organizations of Treadway Commission (COSO), proposed guidelines on risk management and internal control. The COSO framework is a popular model that includes (Apostolou et al., 2014; Moeller, 2011; Smith and Smith, 2016):

1. Control environment - company board sets the integrity and ethical values, management philosophy and directions,
2. Risk assessment - managers set control objectives by conducting risk analysis
3. Control activities - control policies and procedures are proposed and implemented by employees that include performance review, application controls, general control and separation of duties.
4. Information and communication - information collection, documentation, storage, and distribution. This also includes identifying an understanding of responsibilities and roles, as well as communication procedures.

5. Monitoring – managers monitor and improve internal control policies and implementations.

The COSO website provides further updates and free online materials (www.coso.org).

Chapter 5
Revenue Cycle

The purpose of the revenue cycle is to sell goods and services to customers in return of payment. There are two common types of sales in accounting practice. One is cash and the other is a credit sale. The primary objective of the revenue cycle is to record all accounting transaction and activities. In an Accounting Information System, the revenue cycle also provides business process and transaction activities that include (1) sale order, (2) shipping, (3) billing and (4) cash collection (see Figure 3) (Simkin et al., 2014; Romney and Steinbart, 2017; Turner, 2013; Richardson et al., 2013; Smith and Smith, 2016).

Figure 3: Revenue Cycle

In a system flow chart, there are many business transactions. An example of a sale process is shown in Figure 4 (Gelinas et al., 2014; Hurt, 2015; Hall, 2015; Turner, 2013; Richardson et al., 2013; Romney and Steinbart, 2017). The process involves a customer making a sales order, credit check being verified with the bank and/or approved by the company. Once the sale order is approved, the billing system updates records and accounts receivable journals automatically. A copy of the shipping request is sent to the warehouse. The order is packed and shipped by the delivery company. All records are updated and filed in each stage of the sale process accordingly. There are many business process designs; each company has its own process according its operations. However, all financial records and statements are compiled in accordance with

the GAAP, accounting standards, and regulation requirements
(Vanhoof et al., 2016; Turner, 2013; Simkin et al., 2014).

Figure 4: System Flow Chart

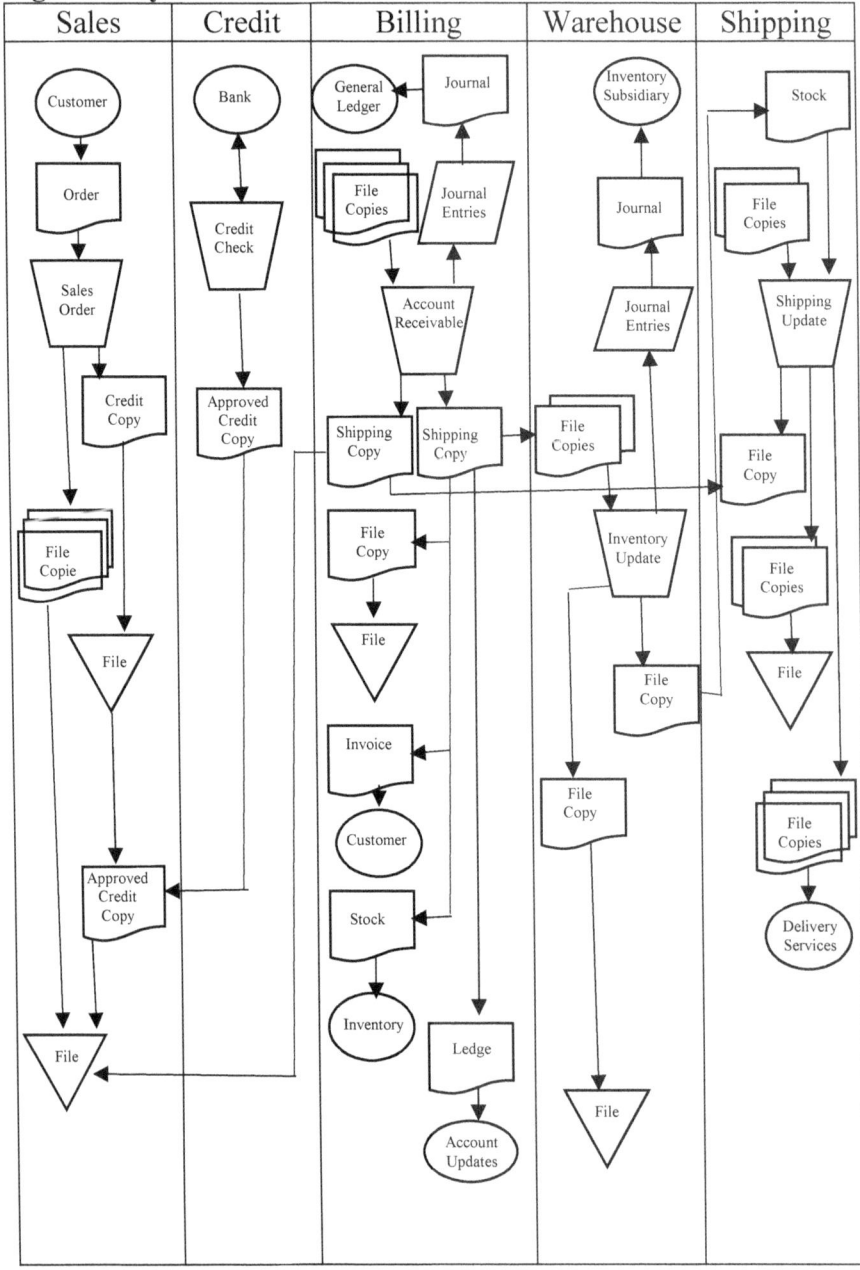

Risks and Controls

Sales

In a sale order, there could be many risks if there is a lack of internal control. Risks include inaccurate, incomplete, and invalid orders, as well as out of stock orders and credit issues with the customer. Internal controls must be carefully designed in accordance with the nature of the sales and business process. For example, reducing security and credit check procedures for long-term regular customers can improve effectiveness and efficiency of the business process (Simkin et al., 2014). Segregation of duties and workflow controls can also reduce risks for an authorized transaction (Richardson et al., 2013). Other internal physical and process control strategies include data entry edit controls, access controls, stock check (i.e. periodic physical inventory count), credit limits and history check for accounts receivable, automation of digital inputs (e.g. barcode), analytical reports from audit logs, and a Customer Relationship Management (CRM) system (Vanhoof et al., 2016; Apostolou et al., 2014; Hall, 2015; Romney and Steinbart, 2017).

Shipping

After a sale order transaction is approved, the warehouse will initiate delivery services and packaging of the inventory, assigning a handling shipping company (carrier) and re-stocking process. The shipping process activities include (1) picking and packing the sale order, and (2) shipping the order (Gelinas et al., 2014, Hurt, 2015; Turner, 2013).

Shipping risks include human errors (e.g. incorrect packing of items and quality, incorrect address, failure to ship) and shipping issues such as delay, lost or stolen packages, accidents, or damage during transportation. Internal control approaches for shipping include an integration system between the sale, warehouse, and carrier services, tracking system, use of barcode, documentations, workflow controls and segregation of duties, reconciliation of sale orders, picking lists and slips, separation of warehouse and shipping services (Simkin et al., 2014; Romney and Steinbart, 2017; Richardson et al., 2013; Hall, 2015; Turner, 2013).

Billing
In billing processes, the two main activities are sending an invoice to the customer and updating accounts receivable (Gelinas et al., 2014). Most billing errors are associated with employees. These errors are incorrect account details, failure to bill, failure to monitor payment due dates, bad debts, or errors occurring during posting in accounts receivable. Effective methods for internal controls are separation of duties reconciliations (e.g. (1) sale orders, shipping and picking lists, (2) batch total, (3) subsidiary accounts to general ledger), and monthly audit reports (e.g. comparing sales, inventory and accounts receivable) (Axelsen et al., 2017; Hall, 2015). With the access controls and integration systems between sale, billing, warehouse, and shipping, billing risks can be reduced significantly (Turner, 2013; Romney and Steinbart, 2017; Richardson et al., 2013; Simkin ct al., 2014;).

Cash Collection
When customers arrange cash payment for the sales orders, the potential threats for cash collection are employees' errors (incorrectly counting the cash), theft, cash flow, and storage (Smith and Smith, 2016). Internal controls for cash collection can be done by segregation of duties, workflow controls (e.g. separation of cash handling functions, assigning two persons to accounting the cash, routine changes of cashiers and transportation persons), reduced amount of cash in-house, use of lockboxes, deposits of large amounts of cash to a bank daily or regularly, maintaining low cash flow in the cash register or point-of-sale system, reconciliation of bank and cash accounts, and security training to handle thefts and accidents (Hall, 2015; Turner, 2013; Romney and Steinbart, 2017; Richardson et al., 2013; Simkin et al., 2014).

Chapter 6

The Expenditure Cycle

The objective of the expenditure cycle is to minimize the costs of purchasing inventories, salaries, supplies, and various internal and external function services (Yong and Moyes, 2014; Coyne et al., 2016). The primary activity of the expenditure cycle is processing transactions from purchase to payment of goods and services. Figure 5 shows an expenditure cycle related activities (Apostolou et al., 2014; Richardson et al., 2013; Romney and Steinbart, 2017; Smith and Smith, 2016).

Figure 5: Expenditure Cycle and Related Activities

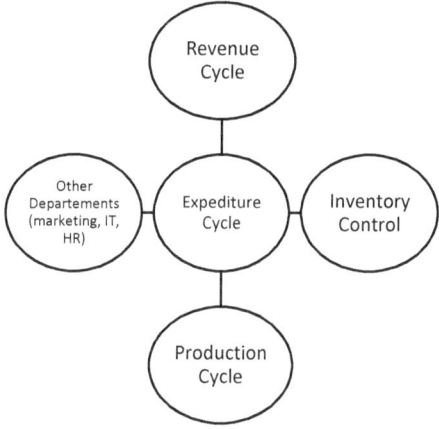

Four expenditure cycle process activities include (see Figure 6) (Coyn et al., 2016; Gelinas et al., 2014; Romney and Steinbart, 2017):

1. Make a purchase order
2. Receive goods
3. Approve incoming invoices from suppliers
4. Pay vendor

Figure 6: Expenditure Cycle

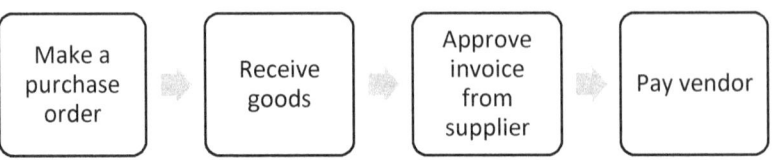

Risks and Controls

General

Data processing and protecting master data are general concerns in internal control (Simkin et al., 2014).

The general internal control for an expenditure cycle can be done by implementing data processing integrity control, authorization and access control, and reviewing changes of the master database (Gelinas et al., 2014; Turner, 2013; Romney and Steinbart, 2017).

Order

Common risks related to ordering include incorrect purchasing records, overstocking, overpricing poor quality inventory, purchasing from unreliable and/or unauthorized suppliers, and kickbacks (Hall, 2015; Turner, 2013).

Control strategies for order include implementation of a perpetual inventory system, use of bar codes, stock-take, verity of purchase requisitions and orders, use of a control price list and competitive bidding system, purchasing process controls, set budgets and sales targets, verify of all suppliers and use of approved suppliers, use automation tracking system, validation of actual delivered items, applied security policies, review hiring employees and regular training, job rotation, and implementation of internal audits (Axelsen et al., 2017; Hall, 2015; Turner, 2013; Romney and Steinbart, 2017; Smith and Smith, 2016).

Receiving

Accepting unordered inventory, miscounting the quantity, incorrectly verifying receipt of services, and theft of inventory are the common issues during the receiving process (Richardson et al., 2013; Simkin et al., 2014).

The internal controls for receiving include requiring employees to sign, check, count, and approve the delivery inventory; implementation of separation of duties; audits; using integration systems such as ERP, bar code; periodical stock-take; and documentation of all receiving processes (Turner, 2013; Richardson et al., 2013; Axelsen et al., 2017).

Approving

Two risks of the approving process are incorrect information of suppliers' invoices and mistakes in posting to accounts payable (Turner, 2013; Hall, 2015).

Internal control strategies for approving include documentations, checking invoice accuracy, review purchase order versus receiving reports; master data access and data entry controls; reconciliation of account payable and general ledger; and use of logistic channels (Hall, 2015; Richardson et al., 2013).

Cash Disbursement

Using a voucher system, a disbursement voucher is created when a supplier invoice is approved for payment. It identifies the supplier, lists the unpaid invoices, and indicates the amount to be paid after deducting any applicable discounts (Masrek et al., 2013; Yong and Moyes, 2014). The benefits of the voucher system are that it can reduce a number of checks, utilize pre-sequential-number voucher control, and allow for separation of invoice approval for the invoice payment (Richardson et al., 2013; Romney and Steinbart, 2017; Simkin et al., 2014).

Threats for cash disbursement can be classified as duplicate payments, insufficient cash flow, alternation of cash payment, failure of receiving discounts, theft of cash, payment alteration, and payment made with no inventory delivery (Hall, 2015; Turner, 2013).

Internal control strategies include a cash flow budget plan, scheduling payment for the discount rate, checking the consistency of documentation (e.g. invoice match inventory level), reviewing receipts for travel expenses, applying corporate credit cards for work expenses, using a voucher system for all payments, reviewing original receipts, access control for cash registers, separation of duties (e.g. issuing bank check and account payable function), physical security monitoring of all issued and blank bank checks, reconciliation of bank statements and cash disbursements, access control of supplier master data, and auditing the petty cash fund (Jayakumari et al., 2017; Yong and Moyes, 2014; Turner, 2013; Romney and Steinbart, 2017; Smith and Smith, 2016).

Chapter 7

Payroll Cycle

The history of accounting information systems began in the early 1970s with the payroll function (Drum et al., 2017; Rom and Rohde, 2007; Gelinas et al., 2014). The payroll cycle is one of the critical areas of accounting. The payroll cycle also provides effective management for human resources. A typical payroll cycle includes a set of processes (i.e. recruiting, training, job duties, employee benefits and compensation, performance review and employee discharges) (Lam et al., 2017; Sledgianowski et al., 2016). Figure 7 illustrates the interconnection between a payroll system and its stakeholders (Smith and Smith, 2016; Hurt, 2015; Hall, 2015; Turner, 2013; Romney and Steinbart, 2017).

Figure 7: Payroll system

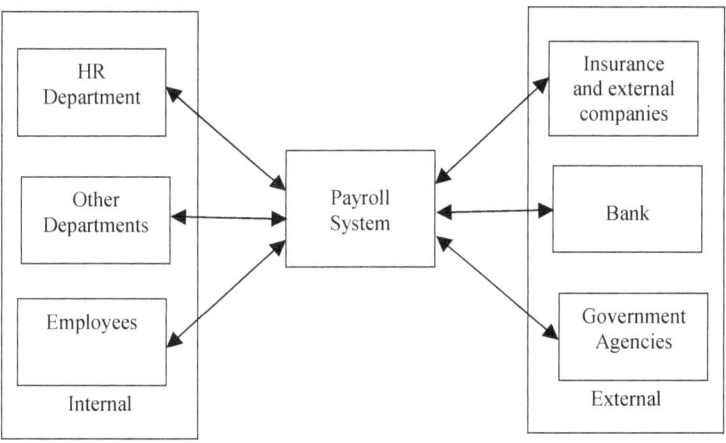

The payroll cycle includes several processes and activities that include master file maintenance, validation of attendance, payroll preparation and distribution, tax preparation and miscellaneous deductions (Hall, 2015; Turner, 2013; Smith and Smith, 2016).

Risks and Controls

General

General risks of a payroll system include an inaccurate master data file, unauthorized access, disclosure of sensitive information, hiring unqualified employees, violation of employment laws, and lost data (Sledgianowski et al., 2016; Gelinas et al., 2014).

General internal control can be done by multiple methods that include data processes and access controls, master file control (including data backup), use of data encryption, and implementation of security procedures, such as hiring procedures, employee background checks, and documentation of employee activities (e.g. qualifications, experiences, performance reviews, and dismissal procedures) (Wong, 2017; Turner, 2013; Richardson et al., 2013).

Master File

Two common risks for updating a master file include incorrect and unauthorized changes of the payroll master files (Smith and Smith, 2016; Hall, 2015).

There are many internal control strategies for updating the master file including segregation of duties (e.g. accounting department manages payroll while HR manages the master file), access controls for all employees, data process controls, and validation of the payroll master file (Turner, 2013; Richardson et al., 2013; Simkin et al., 2014).

Validation

Many operating and retail service companies are generally required to validate work hours and attendance (Simkin et al., 2014; Smith and Smith, 2016). The validation risk becomes an issue.

Validation control strategies can include clock-in and clock-out attendance time cards, biometric authentication for higher security control, and segregation of duties (e.g. comparing records of job-time and time cards and supervisory review) (Romney and Steinbart, 2017; Gelinas et al., 2014; Hall, 2015).

Payroll Preparation
The main risk during the payroll preparation is processing errors. Several internal control techniques can be used for processing errors that include data processing controls, issue earning statements to employees, use of payroll and regulation guidelines and supervisory review (Gelinas et al., 2014; Turner, 2013; Simkin et al., 2014;).

Disburse Payroll
Fraudulent distribution of paychecks is the main concern for the disbursement of payroll (Richardson et al., 2013; Romney and Steinbart, 2017).

Strategies of internal controls can be used for disbursing payroll, including access control to the EFT system, master payroll file, blank checks and check signature machine, segregation of duties of the disbursement payroll process, implementation of security policies and guidelines, reconciliation of bank statements and payroll records, review of unclaimed paychecks and review all EFT transactions and payroll checks (Smith and Smith, 2016; Hall, 2015; Turner, 2013; Romney and Steinbart, 2017).

Disburse Taxes
Common risks of disbursing taxes include failure to provide valid payments, and incorrect or inaccurate payments (Richardson et al., 2013; Hall, 2015).

Internal control strategies for disbursing taxes include implementation of processing integrity controls, supervisory review, and use of Internal Revenue Service (IRS) guidelines for payment (Hurt, 2015; Smith and Smith, 2016; Turner, 2013; Romney and Steinbart, 2017; Simkin et al., 2014).

Chapter 8

Production Cycle

The production cycle is a manufacturing process of raw materials to finished goods. The main activities in a production cycle include designing goods, planning & scheduling, production operations, and cost accounting (see Figure 8) (Ivanov et al., 2016; Gurd and Helliar, 2016; Romney and Steinbart, 2017; Simkin et al., 2014).

Figure 8: Production Process and Activities

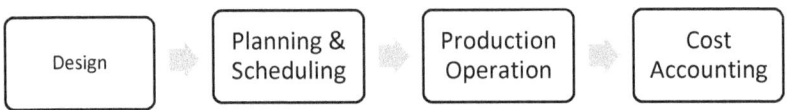

Risks and Controls

General

General risks associated with the production cycle include inaccurate master data or master data error, unauthorized disclosure, and loss of data (Hall, 2015; Richardson et al., 2013).

Control strategies that can be used include accessing and processing integrity control, encryption of sensitive data, review of all updates or changes of master data, regular backup and implementation of a risk management plan (Gelinas et al., 2014; Turner, 2013; Romney and Steinbart, 2017; Simkin et al., 2014).

Design

Poorly designed products might result in additional production costs that are greater than the budget. Accounting analysis of design costs and repair and replacement during warranty are the common techniques for controls (Sledgianowski et al., 2016; Hall, 2015; Turner, 2013; Simkin et al., 2014).

Planning and Scheduling

Delay of production or over production can increase risks during the production cycle. Control techniques and strategies that can be used include planning and scheduling, approval of production process and schedule, implementation of project management plan and tools, and monitoring quality and production risks (Richardson et al., 2013; Romney and Steinbart, 2017).

Production Operations

There is a high degree of risk associated with operation. These threats and risks include theft of fixed assets and current assets (e.g. inventory), poor performance, natural disaster, disruption of raw material supply, and operation errors (Richardson et al., 2013; Smith and Smith, 2016).

To address the production operation risks, many internal control strategies can be used that include documentation of inventory, segregation of duties, access control in data and physical access control, regular stock taking and reconciliation of the physical and master files, auditing, approval of fixed asset acquisition and suppliers of raw materials, production performance evaluation, insurance, backup and risk management plans, physical safeguards, and education of employees (Simkin et al., 2014; Richardson et al., 2013; Hall, 2015; Turner, 2013; Romney and Steinbart, 2017).

Cost Accounting

Risks associated with cost accounting include misleading and incorrect reports, cost data errors, and inaccurate allocations of overhead costs (Hall, 2015; Richardson et al., 2013).

Control techniques that can be used include data processing integrity controls, use of automation of computing system (e.g. barcode), calculate activity cost accounting, job order and process costing, identify cost drivers, and review performance metrics (Turner, 2013; Richardson et al., 2013; Smith and Smith, 2016).

Chapter 9

General Ledger

In the accounting cycle, the general ledger is a consolidated process for all accounting activities (e.g. revenue, expenditure, and payroll), other financial activities (e.g. investment, budgeting, adjustments, financial loans), and reports relevant to stakeholders (Rosen, 2016; Richardson et al., 2013). Figure 9 shows the relationship between the general ledger and reporting system, and other accounting activities (Hall, 2015; Sledgianowski et al., 2016; Turner, 2013; Romney and Steinbart, 2017; Simkin et al., 2014; Smith and Smith, 2016).

Figure 9: General Ledger and Reporting System

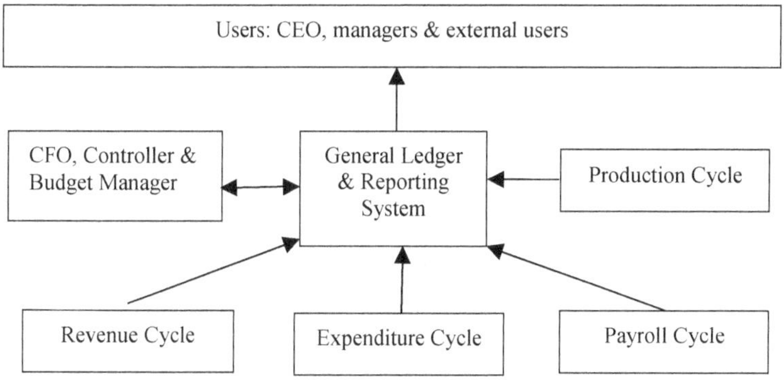

The process of general ledger and reporting activities include updating the general ledger, adjusting entries, preparing financial statements, and management reporting (see Figure 10) (Hurt, 2015; Hall, 2015; Richardson et al., 2013; Romney and Steinbart, 2017; Simkin et al., 2014; Smith and Smith, 2016).

Figure 10: General Ledger and Reporting Process

| Update General Ledger | Post Adjusting Entries | Prepare Financial Statement | Management Reporting |

Risks and Controls

General

Three common risks of general ledger and reporting are incorrect information recorded in the general ledger, lost accounting data, and unauthorized disclosure of financial statements (Sledgianowski et al., 2016; Romney and Steinbart, 2017).

Internal control strategies for general ledger and reporting include access control, data encryption techniques, backups of the master file, use of data processing control policies, and monitoring changes of the general ledger master file (Hurt, 2015; Gelinas et al., 2014; Turner, 2013; Romney and Steinbart, 2017; Simkin et al., 2014).

Updating

Unauthorized and inaccurate updating of journal entries are critical security risks in a general ledger (Richardson et al., 2013; Smith and Smith, 2016).

For internal controls, applying access control and data entry processing integration control, reconciliations of accounts and control reports, and an auditing trail can be used to control the updating of the general ledger (Hurt, 2015; Turner, 2013; Romney and Steinbart, 2017; Smith and Smith, 2016).

Posting

Incorrect and unauthorized adjusting of entries are the key threats to the internal control (Richardson et al., 2013).

Strategies for avoiding these risks include access controls, reconciliations, data entry processing controls, audit trails and adjusting entries (Axelsen et al., 2017; Hall, 2015; Richardson et al., 2013).

Preparing Financial Statements

When preparing financial statements, incorrect, inaccurate, and fraudulent financial statements are the key threats to internal control (Turner, 2013; Smith and Smith, 2016).

Strategies such as applying processing integrity control policies, using accounting information systems, and auditing are internal control methods for preparing financial statements (Drum et al., 2017; Hall, 2015; Richardson et al., 2013; Romney and Steinbart, 2017).

Reporting

There are few risks in reporting. However, poorly designed reports are unacceptable to management (Romney and Steinbart, 2017; Smith and Smith, 2016).

Ways for producing quality management report controls can depend on accounting responsibilities, balanced scorecards, and use of professional graphic design (Gelinas et al., 2014; Turner, 2013).

An accounting information system can produce a balanced scorecard that provides a multidimensional perspective of a company's performance (Hurt, 2015). The balanced scorecard shows the relationship between the target goals and actual performance. Performance indicators such as financial, customer, internal operations, research and development and other relevant performance indicators aid in this perspective (Smith and Smith, 2016; Hall, 2015; Richardson et al., 2013; Romney and Steinbart, 2017).

Reference

Apostolou, B., Dorminey J.W. and Hassell J.M. (2014) A Summary and Analysis of Education Research in Accounting Information Systems (AIS), Journal of Accounting Education. (32)2, 99-112.

Axelsen M., Green P., Ridley G. (2017) Explaining the Information Systems Auditor Role in The Public Sector Financial Audit, Journal of Accounting Information Systems. 24, 15-31.

Bacic D. and Fadlalla A. (2016), Business Information Visualization Intellectual Contributions: An Integrative Framework of Visualization Capabilities and Dimensions of Visual Intelligence, Decision Support Systems, 89, 77-86.

Belfo F. and Trigo A. (2013). Accounting Information Systems: Tradition and Future Director Procedia Technology, CENTERIS Conference 2013, 9, 536-546.

Bhimani A. and Willcocks L. (2014) Accounting and Business Research, Digitisation, 'Big Data' and the Transformation of Accounting Information, Journal of Accounting and Business Research, 44(4), 469-490.

Bol J.C., Kramer S., Maas V.S. (2016) How Control System Design Affects Performance Evaluation Compression: The Role of Information Accuracy and Outcome Transparency, Accounting, Organization and Society. 51, 64-73.

Brahima, S. (2014) ICT Facts and Figures, The International Telecommunication Union, available URL: http://www.itu.int/en/ITU-D/Statistics/Documents/facts/ICTFactsFigures2014-e.pdf

Cassidy A. (2016) A Practical Guide to Information Systems Strategic Planning, Taylor and Francis, New York.

Christ M.H. and Nicolaou A.I (2016) Integrated Information Systems, Alliance Formation, and the Risk of Information

Exchange between Partners, Journal of Management Accounting, 28(3), 1-18.

Collier P.M. (2015). Accounting for managers: Interpreting Accounting Information for Decision Making, Wiley Publisher.

Coyne, J.G. Coyne E.M. and Walker K.B. (2016) A Model to Update Accounting Curricular for Emerging Technologies, Innovation in Education, 13(1). 161-169.

Drum D., Pernsteiner A., Revak A. (2017) Workaround in an SAP Environment: Impacts on Accounting Information Quality, Journal of Accounting & Organizational Change, online: URL: http://www.emeraldinsight.com/doi/abs/10.1108/JAOC-05-2015-0040

Fang J. and Shu L. (2016). Modern Accounting Information System Security (AISS) Research Based on IT Technology. Advanced Science and Technology Letters (AST 2016). vol.121, pp.163-170.

Fawcett M. and Martin D. (2016). Accounting Information Systems. Forest Lodge: Better Teams Publications.

Filsaraei, M. Khakbaz E., Riazi A. (2016) An Overview of Human Resource Accounting in Manufacturing Companies, American Journal of Marketing Research, vol2 (4), 103-113.

Gelinas U.J., Dull R.B. and Wheeler P. (2014) Accounting Information Systems 10th Edition, Cengage Learning.

Gurd B. and Helliar C. (2016) Looking for Leaders: 'Balancing' Innovation Risk and Management Control Systems, The British Accounting Review, 49(1), 91-102.

Hall J.A. (2015) Accounting Information Systems, 9th edition, South-Western College Publisher.

Hayek A., Machmur B., Schreiber M. (2014) 'Safety on a Chip' Turnkey Solution for Industrial Control, Proceedings of IEEE

International Conference on Application-Specific Systems, Architectures and Processors, Zurich, Switzerland, 18-20 June.

Hurt, R. (2015) Accounting Information Systems: Basic Concepts and Current Issues, Fourth Edition, McGraw-Hill.

Ivanov D., Tsipoulanidis A and Schonberger J. (2016) Basic of Supply Chain and Operation Management, In: Global Supply Chain and Operations Management, 1-14.

Jauakumari A.G., Vijaykumar S. (2017) Cash Management – A Recurrent Necessity for Business Growth, Indian Journal of Applied Research, 6(9).

Lam M., Guo H., McGee P. (2017) Accounting Toward Sweet Success: Treadwell's Ice Cream, The Case Journal.

Laudon K.C. and Laudon J.P. (2015) Managing Information Systems: Managing the Digital Firm, 14th Edition, Pearson.

Masrek M.N., Mohamed I.S., Daud N.M. (2014) Internal Financial Controls Practices of District Mosques in Central Region of Malaysia, International Journal of Trade, Economics and Finance; Singapore 5.3, 255-258.

Mayberry M. D. (2013). CAATTs Ideal for Efficient Audits. American Institute of CPAs (accessed 6 Jan 2016).

Moeller R.R. (2011) COSO Enterprise Risk Management, Establishing Effective Governance, Risk, and Compliance Process, 2nd Edition: John Wiley & Sons.

Rom A. and Rohde C. (2007). Management Accounting and Integrated Information Systems: A Literature Review, International Journal of Accounting Information Systems, 8, pp40-68.

Romney M. B. and Steinbart P.J. (2017) Accounting Information Systems. 14th Edition. Pearson.

Rosen B (2016) Best Practices for Accounting Procedures for Micro, Small and Medium-Sized Businesses, Ariz. J. Int;l & Comp. L., available on: HeinOline.

Richardson V., Chang C. and Smith R. (2013) Accounting Information Systems, 1st Edition. McGraw-Hill.

Sledgianowski D., Gomaa M. and Tan C. (2017) Toward Integration of Big Data, Technology and Information Systems Competencies into the Accounting Curriculum, Journal of Accounting Education. In press, on-line version URL: http://www.sciencedirect.com/science/article/pii/S0748575116301282

Simkin M.G., Norman C.S. and Rose J.M. (2014). Core Concepts of Accounting Information Systems. 13th Edition. Wiley.

Smith M. and Smith K.T. (2016) Accounting Information Systems, 5th Edition. CreateSpace Independent Publishing Platform

Singh K. (2016), Implementing Enterprise Resource Planning Education in a Postgraduate Accounting Information Systems Course, Business Education & Accreditation, 8(1), 27-37.

Sutcliffe, A.G., Van Assche, F., and Denyon D., (2016) Domain Knowledge for Interactive System Design, Springer.

Stede Van der W. and Malone R. (2010) Accounting Trends in a Borderless World., Chartered Institute of Management Accountants.

Turner L. (2013) Accounting Information Systems: The Controls and Process. 2nd Edition. Wiley.

Vanhoof E., De Bruyn P., Aerts W and Verelst J. (2016) Building An Evolvable Prototype for a Multiple GAAP Accounting Information System, Lecture Notes in Business Information Processing, Advances in Enterprise Engineering X, 252, 71-85.

Ward J. and Peppard J. (2016) The Strategic Management of Information Systems: Building a Digital Strategy, Wiley.

Wikipedia, (2016). List of Countries by Number of Mobile Phones in Use, 29 Oct. 2016.

Wong Y.K. (2017) Cyber Security and Accounting Information Systems, Orlando: FL. ISBN: 1541312430 / 9781541312432

Yong R. and Moyes, G.D. (2014) An examination of the effectiveness of test-of-controls audit procedures for detecting fraud, International Journal Auditing, 2(1), 22-36.

www.ingramcontent.com/pod-product-compliance
Lightning Source LLC
Chambersburg PA
CBHW061226180526
45170CB00003B/1172